MALMESBURY

PHOTOGRAPHIC MEMORIES

ROBERTA PRINCE has lived for many years in a variety of beautiful and historically interesting towns and villages throughout the Cotswolds, which have stimulated her love of the countryside and its history. Having originally become involved in museums through her career as a graphic designer/display assistant, she eventually became the curator of the Athelstan Museum in Malmesbury in 1983. Over the years Roberta has worked closely with the local community, assisting visitors to the museum, both from the UK and overseas, with their family history research and also assisting professional researchers with research into Malmesbury's unique history. Her particular interest and research has been into the Malmesbury lace industry and in promoting awareness of the craft to the general public. Roberta has many different interests and enjoys sailing, painting, reading, yoga and attending vintage car trials with her husband and their old MG car.

FRANCIS FRITH'S
PHOTOGRAPHIC MEMORIES

MALMESBURY

PHOTOGRAPHIC MEMORIES

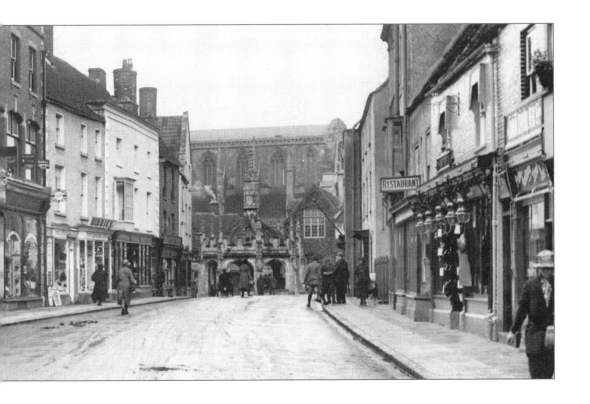

ROBERTA PRINCE

First published in paperback in the United Kingdom in
2004 by Frith Book Company Ltd

Text and Design copyright © Frith Book Company Ltd
Photographs copyright © The Francis Frith Collection

British Library Cataloguing in Publication Data

Francis Frith's Malmesbury - Photographic Memories
Roberta Prince
ISBN 1-85937-858-7

Frith Book Company Ltd
Frith's Barn, Teffont,
Salisbury, Wiltshire SP3 5QP
Tel: +44 (0) 1722 716 376
Email: info@francisfrith.co.uk
www.francisfrith.co.uk

Printed and bound in Great Britain

Front Cover: **MALMESBURY**, *Market Cross 1924* 76146t
Frontispiece: **MALMESBURY**, *High Street 1924* 76144
2004 photographs by Roberta Prince

*The colour-tinting is for illustrative purposes only, and is not intended
to be historically accurate*

Acknowledgements
The author wishes to acknowledge with thanks the following people who have assisted her in producing the book:
Mr Tim Porter, medieval historian, for recommending that she should undertake the writing of the book.
Her husband, Jeremy, for his valuable assistance with some of the typing and proof reading.
The Athelstan Museum and Wiltshire County Council Museum Service for supplying the extra photographs from
the Athelstan Museum archives.
Also she wishes to acknowledge 'The Victoria History of Wiltshire, Volume XIV, Malmesbury Hundred', which has
been a valuable reference, along with various archive materials from the museum.

CONTENTS

FRANCIS FRITH
VICTORIAN PIONEER

FRANCIS FRITH, founder of the world-famous photographic archive, was a complex and multi-talented man. A devout Quaker and a highly successful Victorian businessman, he was philosophical by nature and pioneering in outlook.

By 1855 he had already established a wholesale grocery business in Liverpool, and sold it for the astonishing sum of £200,000, which is the equivalent today of over £15,000,000. Now a very rich man, he was able to indulge his passion for travel. As a child he had pored over travel books written by early explorers, and his fancy and imagination had been stirred by family holidays to the sublime mountain regions of Wales and Scotland. 'What lands of spirit-stirring and enriching scenes and places!' he had written. He was to return to these scenes of grandeur in later years to 'recapture the thousands of vivid and tender memories', but with a different purpose. Now in his thirties, and captivated by the new science of photography, Frith set out on a series of pioneering journeys up the Nile and to the Near East that occupied him from 1856 until 1860.

INTRIGUE AND EXPLORATION

These far-flung journeys were packed with intrigue and adventure. In his life story, written when he was sixty-three, Frith tells of being held captive by bandits, and of fighting 'an awful midnight battle to the very point of surrender with a deadly pack of hungry, wild dogs'. Wearing flowing Arab costume, Frith arrived at Akaba by camel sixty years before Lawrence of Arabia, where he encountered 'desert princes and rival sheikhs, blazing with jewel-hilted swords'.

He was the first photographer to venture beyond the sixth cataract of the Nile. Africa was still the mysterious 'Dark Continent', and Stanley and Livingstone's historic meeting was a decade into the future. The conditions for picture taking confound belief. He laboured for hours in his wicker dark-room in the sweltering heat of the desert, while the volatile chemicals fizzed dangerously in their trays. Back in London he exhibited his photographs and was 'rapturously cheered' by members of the Royal Society. His reputation as a photographer was made overnight.

VENTURE OF A LIFE-TIME

Characteristically, Frith quickly spotted the opportunity to create a new business as a specialist publisher of photographs. He lived in an era of immense and sometimes violent change.

For the poor in the early part of Victoria's reign work was exhausting and the hours long, and people had precious little free time to enjoy themselves. Most had no transport other than a cart or gig at their disposal, and rarely travelled far beyond the boundaries of their own town or village. However, by the 1870s the railways had threaded their way across the country, and Bank Holidays and half-day Saturdays had been made obligatory by Act of Parliament. All of a sudden the working man and his family were able to enjoy days out and see a little more of the world.

With typical business acumen, Francis Frith foresaw that these new tourists would enjoy having souvenirs to commemorate their days out. In 1860 he married Mary Ann Rosling and set out on a new career: his aim was to photograph every city, town and village in Britain. For the next thirty years he travelled the country by train and by pony and trap, producing fine photographs of seaside resorts and beauty spots that were keenly bought by millions of Victorians. These prints were painstakingly pasted into family albums and pored over during the dark nights of winter, rekindling precious memories of summer excursions.

THE RISE OF FRITH & CO

Frith's studio was soon supplying retail shops all over the country. To meet the demand he gathered about him a small team of photographers, and published the work of independent artist-photographers of the calibre of Roger Fenton and Francis Bedford. In order to gain some understanding of the scale of Frith's business one only has to look at the catalogue issued by Frith & Co in 1886: it runs to some 670 pages, listing not only many thousands of views of the British Isles but also many photographs of most European countries, and China, Japan, the USA and Canada - note the sample page shown on page 9 from the hand-written Frith & Co ledgers recording the pictures. By 1890 Frith had created the greatest specialist photographic publishing company in the world, with over 2,000 sales outlets - more than the combined number that Boots and WH Smith have today! The picture on the next page shows the Frith & Co display board at Ingleton in the Yorkshire Dales (left of window). Beautifully constructed with a mahogany frame and gilt inserts, it could display up to a dozen local scenes.

POSTCARD BONANZA

The ever-popular holiday postcard we know today took many years to develop. In 1870 the Post Office issued the first plain cards, with a pre-printed stamp on one face. In 1894 they allowed other publishers' cards to be sent through the mail with an attached adhesive halfpenny stamp. Demand grew rapidly, and in 1895 a new size of postcard was permitted called the court card, but there was little room for illustration. In 1899, a year after Frith's death, a new card measuring 5.5 x 3.5 inches became the standard format, but it was not until 1902 that the divided back came into being, so that the address and message could be on one face and a full-size illustration on the other. Frith & Co were in the vanguard of postcard development: Frith's sons Eustace and Cyril continued their father's monumental task, expanding the number of views offered to the public and recording more and more places in Britain, as the coasts and countryside were opened up to mass travel.

Francis Frith had died in 1898 at his villa in Cannes, his great project still growing. The archive he created continued in business for another seventy years. By 1970 it contained over a third of a million pictures showing 7,000 British towns and villages.

FRANCIS FRITH'S LEGACY

Frith's legacy to us today is of immense significance and value, for the magnificent archive of evocative photographs he created provides a unique record of change in the cities, towns and villages throughout Britain over a century and more. Frith and his fellow studio photographers revisited locations many times down the years to update their views, compiling for us an enthralling and colourful pageant of British life and character.

We are fortunate that Frith was dedicated to recording the minutiae of everyday life. For it is this sheer wealth of visual data, the painstaking chronicle of changes in dress, transport, street layouts, buildings, housing, engineering and landscape that captivates us so much today. His remarkable images offer us a powerful link with the past and with the lives of our ancestors.

THE VALUE OF THE ARCHIVE TODAY

Computers have now made it possible for Frith's many thousands of images to be accessed almost instantly. Frith's images are increasingly used as visual resources, by social historians, by researchers into genealogy and ancestry, by architects and town planners, and by teachers involved in local history projects.

In addition, the archive offers every one of us an opportunity to examine the places where we and our families have lived and worked down the years. Highly successful in Frith's own era, the archive is now, a century and more on, entering a new phase of popularity. Historians consider the Francis Frith Collection to be of prime national importance. It is the only archive of its kind remaining in private ownership. Francis Frith's archive is now housed in an historic timber barn in the beautiful village of Teffont in Wiltshire. Its founder would not recognize the archive office as it is today. In place of the many thousands of dusty boxes containing glass plate negatives and an all-pervading odour of photographic chemicals, there are now ranks of computer screens. He would be amazed to watch his images travelling round the world at unimaginable speeds through internet lines.

The archive's future is both bright and exciting. Francis Frith, with his unshakeable belief in making photographs available to the greatest number of people, would undoubtedly approve of what is being done today with his lifetime's work. His photographs depicting our shared past are now bringing pleasure and enlightenment to millions around the world a century and more after his death.

MALMESBURY
AN INTRODUCTION

THE PICTURESQUE historic town of Malmesbury is in North Wiltshire, situated high on a promontory virtually surrounded by the two tributaries of the Bristol Avon. Both tributaries, the Tetbury Avon and the Sherston Avon, converge at the southern end of the town. The river continues its journey through Wiltshire to the Severn estuary at Avonmouth, near Bristol. The town is close to the edge of the Cotswolds, and is part of the Malmesbury hundred, which comprises many estates and villages. Malmesbury was possibly a self-governing borough by the early Middle Ages, and there was a merchants' guild in the town by the 13th century.

The houses in Malmesbury are mainly built of limestone with stone-tiled roofs. Some houses are also limewashed and rendered, and there are also a few red brick buildings. Behind some of the modern shop fronts of the High Street are earlier buildings, and there are 18th-century buildings here too. By the 19th century, new buildings for commercial and civic premises were appearing, such as the Town Hall; it was built in Cross Hayes, where the market, the fairs and various celebrations were held. The Malmesbury Branch Railway opened in 1877.

The fire station was in the Town Hall from 1907 to 1948, when it moved to new premises in Gloucester Road.

EARLY HISTORY

Because of its advantageous defensible position, it had once been suggested that Malmesbury was the site of an Iron Age hillfort. This has now been confirmed: evidence discovered during excavations undertaken in 1998-2000 revealed an extended period of occupation during the early/middle Iron Age, consisting of many phases of construction of ramparts and ditches of the hillfort. There is very little evidence of Roman occupation in Malmesbury, although a hypocaust is said to have been found to the east of the abbey, and various small artefacts have emerged over time. The Athelstan Museum has a collection of Roman artefacts from the Fosse Way excavations undertaken by A D Passmore during the 1930s. There is also a sarcophagus in the museum dating from the Romano-British period, which was discovered on a farm in nearby Sherston in 1987; it contained the remains of a child. More recently, a counterfeit copper coin dating from the 3rd century AD was found at the site of the town walls.

Excavations in 1993 to investigate the town walls confirmed that the defences may have had three phases of construction between the 7th and the 12th centuries. Malmesbury was a burh, or fortified town, at the time of both Alfred the Great and his son Edward the Elder; the town was mentioned in the Burghal Hidage of c900, the document that described the defences of Wessex during the threat of invasion by the Danes. The wall defences in Malmesbury were still extant in the late 13th century. There were five gates leading into the town. The east gate was across Oxford Street in Holloway, Wyniard Gate was a small gate to the south of Silver Street, the south gate was at the southern end of the High Street at the junction with King's Wall, the postern gate was at the junction of King's Wall and Burnivale, and finally the west gate was in Abbey Row. The layout of the town inside the walls, which was mainly established by the late 13th century, remains similar today. The walls survived until the early 16th century, but they received further damage during the Civil War period. Rebuilding of the walls took place in the 18th and 19th centuries.

A mint operated in Malmesbury from the mid 10th century until the late 11th century. This indicates the town's importance at that time; indeed, Malmesbury was recorded in the Domesday Book as a borough of status. Silver coins minted in Malmesbury and dating from the Saxon and Norman periods can be seen in the Athelstan Museum.

MALMESBURY ABBEY

In the 7th century, Mailduib (Maildulph), an Irish monk or hermit, settled in Malmesbury and founded a monastic school. The name Malmesbury may originally have been derived from his name. One of his pupils was Aldhelm (639-709), who became a most learned scholar. Aldhelm's ancestry linked him to the kings of Wessex. He learnt Latin and Greek, wrote poems in English and composed music.

Aldhelm founded the Benedictine monastery at Malmesbury c675 and became the Abbot of Malmesbury, and later Bishop of Sherborne. Aldhelm was revered as a learned man and saint. He died c709 and was buried in Malmesbury abbey. About 837 King Aethelwulf of Wessex made a shrine in the abbey for St Aldhelm's remains. The abbey, dedicated to St Peter and St Paul, became a focus for pilgrimage.

King Athelstan, grandson of Alfred the Great and first king of all England, is reputed to have been buried in Malmesbury Abbey c939. He was a kinsman of St Aldhelm - both men were related to King Ine of Wessex. The whereabouts of Athelstan's remains are uncertain, but according to the historian William of Malmesbury, he was buried near the high altar of St Mary's Church; there is a monumental tomb of a later date dedicated to him in the abbey. King Athelstan was a great benefactor to the abbey and the people of Malmesbury. During the 9th and 10th centuries, Malmesbury was suffering from the Viking raids which were taking place in Wiltshire at that time. It is claimed that the men of Malmesbury assisted King Athelstan in his battles against the Danes, and that he rewarded the alderman and burgesses of the town with certain privileges and five hides of land (700 acres) known as King's Heath, near Norton. The original charter setting out these privileges no longer exists, but later charters supposedly confirmed these claims; the last was c1604, although there is some dispute about the authenticity of these charters. Certainly the land was in the ownership of the Warden and Freemen of the Old Corporation of Malmesbury, who by the 16th century governed the town (except for the abbey) inside the walls; this land would also have included Westport outside the walls. In the 9th century the town was becoming a trading centre and expanding around the abbey.

The abbey's library was renowned throughout Europe during William of Malmesbury's time (c1095-c1143), and indeed before then. William was a revered historian, famous for his 'De Gesta Regum' (the Deeds of the King of England) and 'Gesta Pontificum Anglorum' (the Deeds of the Bishops of England). In 'De Gesta Regum', William refers to the flight undertaken by the monk Eilmer c1010. Eilmer was interested in mathematics and astrology, and in the mechanism of flight. He made some wings and jumped from a tower; he is reputed to have flown some reasonable distance, but he broke both legs when he crashed to the ground. He survived his injuries and lived to a healthy old age.

In the 12th century Roger, Bishop of Salisbury, held Malmesbury Abbey, having deposed Abbot Eadwulf. He then built a castle close to the graveyard of the abbey, possibly on the site of the Old Bell Hotel. In 1153 Henry of Anjou captured the castle, which was garrisoned by King Stephen. By around 1215 the castle was in the keeping of the abbey – the abbey was later given license by the Crown to demolish the castle c1216.

At the Dissolution of the Monasteries around 1539, the abbey was surrendered to Henry VIII; later, Sir Edward Baynton took charge of the abbey. His deputy was William Stumpe, a wealthy clothier of Malmesbury, who eventually purchased the abbey and the monastic buildings from the Crown. The nave of the abbey became Malmesbury's parish church, replacing the ruined St Paul's Church. The other buildings were used as workshops for William Stumpe's looms.

MALMESBURY'S LATER HISTORY

Malmesbury was an important centre for various textile trades. The woollen cloth trade flourished in the 16th century, and there were several different mills operating in the medieval period (there was also a tannery and corn mills). The river encircling the town was a great advantage for fulling the cloth, and the sloping ground to the south of the town was useful for bleaching. By the latter part of the 18th century Malmesbury's lace-making industry was established; it flourished until the mid 19th century, and played an important part in the town's economy. In 1871, there were 35 lace-makers in the town. By the 19th century, when lace was starting to be produced by mechanisation, the cottage industry of handmade lace declined; as prices for the lace decreased, so did the wages of the lace-makers. However, by the mid 19th century the Burton Hill Mill (Avon Mill) was manufacturing silk ribbon, and many lace-makers found employment at the mill.

There was a lace-making revival in the early 20th century instigated by the Countess of Suffolk and Berkshire to ensure that the craft of lace-making would not die out. In 1907 she started a lace school, with lessons being given once a week in the Market Room of the King's Arms Hotel in the High Street. The classes were well

MALMESBURY, *The Lace-making School 1908-09* ZZZ02050
(Photograph courtesy of the Athelstan Museum)

Here we see the pupils of the lace-making school, which was situated in the Market Room of the King's Arms, High Street. From left to right, in the back row are: Elsie Vaughan, Florrie Bishop, Annie Bishop (Mrs Annie Goodfield), May Jacobs, May Tanner. Middle row: Florrie Weeks, Ms Denly, Mrs Jones (proprietress of the King's Arms), Mrs Fisher (teacher), Florrie Drew, Cassie Drew. Front row: Daisy Jefferies, Hilda Fry, Maud Phelps, Nell Jefferies, May Reeves, Eva Jefferies, Kitty Bond.

attended, with the young pupils coming from a wide area around Malmesbury. In 1908 the Countess had a stall at the Daily Mail, 'Exhibition of British Lace', with demonstrations of the craft of Malmesbury lace-making. Many pupils excelled at the craft; one of them was Lizzie Barnes (neé White), who won many awards for her lace-making, and another was Annie Goodfield (neé Bishop), who in her later life demonstrated her work at the Festival of Flowers held in the abbey in the 1960s. A more recent revival has taken place since the 1980s: the curator has arranged demonstrations in the Athelstan Museum, and the book 'Malmesbury Lace' by Joan Blanchard has been published, so that the craft is learnt world wide.

**THE COUNTESS OF SUFFOLK VISITING THE
LACE-MAKING CLASS** *c1910* ZZZ02051
(Reproduced courtesy of the Athelstan Museum)

THE PHILOSOPHER THOMAS HOBBES
(etching, artist unknown) 19th century ZZZ02052
(Reproduced courtesy of the Athelstan Museum)

Further damage to the abbey and town occurred during the Civil War. Malmesbury had submitted to the Royalists, but in March 1643 Sir William Waller captured the town for Parliament. Fierce fighting took place in abbey Row, and all the Royalist commanders and officers and most of the soldiers were taken prisoner. St Mary's Church, Westport was demolished, and the bells were melted down and used to make cannon. There are three letters in the Athelstan Museum written to Prince Rupert at this time, requesting his assistance to help by sending an armed regiment to Malmesbury. Unfortunately help was not forthcoming from him, and Sir William Waller entered the town at Westport. Malmesbury changed sides several times during the war between March 1643 and May 1644. Later, Parliament ordered the destruction of the town walls, thereby ensuring that the town no longer had any strong defences.

The famous philosopher Thomas Hobbes (1588-1679) was born and grew up in the parish of Westport in Malmesbury. His father was vicar of Westport, and is reputed to have left

Malmesbury in disgrace, leaving Thomas in the care of his uncle Francis, who was a prosperous glover in the town. He was educated at Malmesbury school and later, when he was eight years old, he attended Robert Latimer's school in Westport. By the time he came to leave the school at the age of fourteen, he was already a very learned scholar. Thomas Hobbes entered Magdalen Hall, Oxford in 1603. When he graduated he became tutor to William Cavendish, who later became the 2nd Earl of Devonshire. During the 17th century, Hobbes travelled extensively, visiting France, Germany and Italy. At this time he was beginning to be recognised for his philosophical works, particularly his 'Leviathan' and 'De Cive', and for his knowledge of mathematics. Some of his views were very controversial for the times, and caused him to leave the country. He moved to Paris, and whilst there he became tutor of mathematics to the future Charles II. After the Restoration, Thomas Hobbes returned to England and lived with his long-time patron, the Earl of Devonshire. Having left London, he spent the rest of his life at Hardwick Hall and Chatsworth. He died in December 1679, and he is buried in the chancel of Ault Hucknall Church, Derbyshire.

Malmesbury has had a long and interesting association with political personages and events over the centuries. During the 17th century, Sir Lawrence Washington lived in Garsdon Manor, near Malmesbury. He was a descendant of Lawrence Washington of Sulgrave in Northamptonshire, and ancestor to George Washington, the President of America in the late 18th century. Sir Lawrence was a staunch Royalist, and held the position of Register of Chancery; he had been knighted by Charles I in 1627. His portrait, which shows the Washington arms (which feature the 'stars and bars' associated with the American national flag), can be seen in the Athelstan Museum. Another link with American history is through Nancy Hanks, who was the mother of President Abraham Lincoln; her ancestor Thomas Hanks was reputed to have emigrated from Malmesbury to Virginia during the 17th century. The name Hanks was associated with different trades in the town, including those of clockmakers, artist and photographer.

In 1774 Charles James Fox, the third son of Lord Holland, became Member of Parliament for Malmesbury, having previously been elected High Steward in 1769. He was also Lord of the Treasury from 1772 until 1774, and in 1784 was elected MP for Westminster. At the time that he was MP for Malmesbury, Charles James Fox was a supporter of parliamentary reform and the elimination of rotten boroughs, of which Malmesbury was one. He was active in foreign affairs, and opposed North's governmental policy of taxing the American colonists without their agreement. He also believed in the abolition of the slave trade. In 1806 Charles James Fox was appointed Foreign Secretary, but he died later that year on 13 September. The museum has a collection of commemorative artefacts dedicated to him.

Another Member of Parliament and benefactor to the town of Malmesbury was Walter Powell – he was also a keen balloonist. He was born in 1842 in Newport, South Wales, and educated at Rugby School from 1858 until 1861. He moved to North Wiltshire in 1867 and rented Dauntsey House. At this time he joined the local Conservative Association, and in December 1868 he was chosen as the Conservative parliamentary candidate for the borough of Malmesbury. His campaign was successful, and was celebrated at the George Hotel in the town in February 1869. By 1878 Powell had moved to The Old Rectory, Little Somerford; by this time he had become a benefactor to the town of Malmesbury – he was responsible for the building of a reading room and library in Silver Street, erected in 1870. Walter Powell also established the Ragged School, which was situated in Burnivale on land which was given by Thomas Luce, and in 1875 he funded the installation of the gas lighting for the abbey.

Walter Powell was an enthusiastic balloonist, and he had made several successful training flights with his friend Henry Coxwell, who had introduced him to ballooning. In June 1881 Mr Coxwell intended to make an ascent in a balloon with Walter Powell from the Cross Hayes, Malmesbury. Unfortunately, Mr Coxwell was unwell on the appointed day of the flight, so another aeronaut, Mr Thomas Wright, brought his balloon 'Eclipse' to Malmesbury to make the trip instead. This was a great day of celebration for the town, with the crowds gathering in the Cross Hayes to see the ascent of their daring benefactor. The balloon had been filled with gas from the Malmesbury Gas Works by means of some very long pipes which came into the square. The flight was successful, and Walter Powell was then determined to have his own balloon. His balloon was made of silk (probably from the silk mill) and was believed to have been striped red and yellow; it was named 'Daystar'. He had many adventures in the balloon during the year. Then on 9 December 1881, he accompanied another friend, Captain James Templer, and his colleague Mr A Agg-Gardner, on a flight in the Meteorological Office balloon 'Saladin' to measure weather conditions and cloud movements. The weather was very poor when they ascended from Bath in Somerset. Walter Powell managed the balloon, whilst Captain Templer undertook his observations. Unfortunately, owing to the deteriorating weather conditions and the releasing of too much ballast, the balloon (which by this time had reached the Dorset cliffs at Eype) was in trouble, and an emergency landing was the only option. The landing went wrong, and both Captain Templer and Mr Agg-Gardner fell out of the 'Saladin', leaving Walter Powell in the balloon; its load was now considerably lighter, so it ascended rapidly and headed out over the Channel. Walter Powell was never seen again: neither he nor the 'Saladin' were ever found, even after various searches had been undertaken. Malmesbury mourned the sad loss of their pioneering MP.

Malmesbury has had many interesting and inventive people associated with its history. For instance, the museum has a collection of silk posters and a letter advertising Joseph Poole's 'Myriorama'. Joseph Poole lived in Verona House in Gloucester Road, Malmesbury, and he was elected Mayor of Malmesbury twice. The Myriorama was a combination of the earlier dioramas and panoramas with variety acts. The panoramas were scenes painted by artists on canvas, very often depicting historical or topical events. The scenes were moved in front of the spectators, accompanied by music and special lighting effects. A narrator explained the panoramic scenes to the audience. Joseph Poole and his brothers George, Harry, Charles and Fred were all showmen involved with this successful and innovative family touring entertainment busi-

CROSS HAYES *June 1881* ZZZ02053 (Reproduced courtesy of the Athelstan Museum)
The crowds gather to see Walter Powell ascend in Thomas Wright's balloon 'Eclipse'.

ness, either as managers or proprietors, from the 1880s to the early 20th century. The Myrioramas, which were produced in studios in Malmesbury and in London, toured all over the country. With the development of cinema the Myriorama's popularity decreased, and the Poole family became involved with cinema management. Later, in 1935, the Athelstan Cinema was opened; the building was situated near the Market Cross, and it had 333 seats. Sadly, the cinema closed in 1973.

There are many more interesting facts about Malmesbury that could be related, but space is at a premium. I have mainly concentrated on the people and events that have shaped Malmesbury's unique and vibrant past. Malmesbury today is a busy, thriving community, whose population has increased over the years along with the number of visitors to the town. The abbey still remains the focal point in the town, as it has been for centuries. As we can see from the selection of photographs taken in 2004, the traffic has increased, and it was difficult to take these photographs from a similar position to that of the Frith's photographer. In spite of this, the town can easily be compared with the earlier photographs, because Malmesbury has retained the historic layout of the town as well as its individual character.

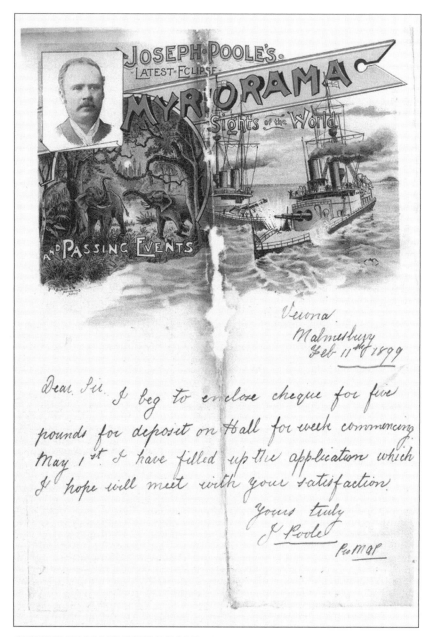

LETTER FROM JOSEPH POOLE *1899* ZZZ02054
(Reproduced courtesy of the Athelstan Museum)

Joseph Poole wrote this letter from his home at Verona House, Malmesbury to book a hall for the showing of his Myriorama.

MALMESBURY ABBEY

As one approaches Malmesbury, the magnificent abbey can be seen high on the hill in the centre of the town. Only a third of the original abbey remains today after the Dissolution of the Monasteries during the reign of Henry VIII. The abbey dates from the late 12th century and it was built in the late Romanesque or Norman style (c1150-1190) with some parts of the abbey being re-built later in the decorated Gothic style. In the late 12th century the newly built abbey was consecrated. It was built in the shape of the cross, and it had a lantern tower surmounted by a spire. This spire was reputed to be higher than that of Salisbury Cathedral; however, in 1479 the spire fell during a storm, causing severe damage to the east end of the abbey. Further damage occurred when the west tower fell in the 17th century and demolished three bays of the nave. The abbey has undergone restoration during 1822 and 1823, in 1903, and between 1926 and 1928. In 1928 the newly restored abbey was re-opened and re-hallowed. Today, Malmesbury Abbey is still a powerful spiritual influence in the town, as it has been for centuries.

MALMESBURY ABBEY AND ABBEY HOUSE *(pencil and grey wash) by Luke Sullivan 1752* ZZZ02055 (Reproduced courtesy of the Athelstan Museum)

This view of Malmesbury Abbey and abbey House is one of four early topographical pencil and grey wash drawings of Malmesbury drawn by the artist Luke Sullivan (c1725-1771), who was a topographical artist, an engraver and a fine watercolour miniaturist. He was the son of a groom to the Duke of Beaufort, whose patronage assisted him to obtain drawing and engraving lessons. He eventually became assistant to William Hogarth, and engraved many important plates of Hogarth's work. At the time that these four drawings were executed, he was the drawing master to the Earl of Suffolk's household at Charlton Park near Malmesbury.

THE ABBEY *c1960* M13042

THE ABBEY *1924* 76149

This fine photograph of Malmesbury Abbey was taken from the north, with the abbey mill buildings below. Just below the abbey we can see the extensive orchard which has now become the Cloister Gardens. Flowing under the charming bridge in the foreground is the River Avon; this tributary is called the Tetbury Avon (it is also known as the Newnton River or the River Ingleburne). The Malmesbury Branch Railway line is situated to the east of the river - the GWR eventually opened this line, which was linked to the Dauntsey Railway, in December 1877. Dauntsey station was opened c1868.

THE ABBEY, *South Side 1924* 76150

In 1903 the main south wall of the abbey was built up to the
ruined west front, and repairs to the roof and buttresses on the
north side and east end were undertaken. The main restoration
took place between 1926 and 1928, when the south transept wall
was repaired.

THE ABBEY *1924* 76151

Here we see the abbey from the south, featuring the great 12th-century south porch with its elaborate figurative carving. The church was repaired during 1822 and 1823 and in 1903. Further restoration was carried out between 1926 and 1928, after this photograph was taken.

THE ABBEY, *The South Porch 1924* 76153

Malmesbury Abbey's unique south porch, dating from the mid 12th century and built in the Romanesque style, is decorated with thirty-eight fine sculptures depicting detailed and elaborate images, some of which are based on Biblical scenes from both the Old and New Testaments. The images are divided by columns with decorative patterns.

23

THE ABBEY
The South Porch 1924 76154

This photograph shows the inside of the porch. Above the doorway is the tympanum, which contains an iconic sculpture of Christ in Majesty seated on a rainbow, holding a book in his left hand and raising his right hand in blessing. A halo shines around Him, supported by a pair of angels. On either side of the porch sit the apostles, six on each side with an angel above holding a scroll. St Peter can be identified holding his key and sitting on Christ's right-hand side. St Paul is opposite. In this photograph we can see some interesting notices. The one to the right of the door is advertising the harvest festival, and another requests visitors to 'place an offering in the abbey Restoration box'. On the notice board on the right are some income tax notices.

Detail of 76154

THE ABBEY RUINS *1924* 76155

This photograph shows the great arch at the eastern end of the abbey. It formed part of the structure above which was built the lantern tower and spire. During a storm in the late 15th century the tower collapsed, causing a great deal of damage. Repairs to the ruined east end were undertaken, and the archway was closed up, which preserved the nave of the church.

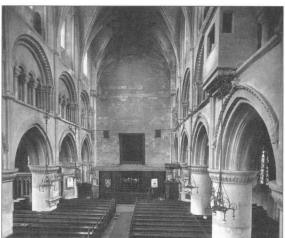

THE ABBEY, *The Nave, looking East 1924* 76158

The nave arcade is built in the late Romanesque style, in which the rounded Norman arches begin to change to the pointed Gothic style. The nave has a stone rood screen of late Perpendicular date. The central doorway is now blocked, and the cornice has the royal arms of Henry VII. Above the screen is a large painting of The Raising of Lazarus, which was presented by the Earl of Suffolk and Berkshire. The arcades have pointed arches with simple bold mouldings supported on cylindrical piers with scalloped capping. The triforium has a semi-circular arch in each bay with zigzag moulding inside each arch, and on the small pillars are four smaller arches. The square structure on the south side of the nave is known as the Watching Loft; its origins and purpose are not certain. It has been suggested that it was used by the monastic community to either relay their ceremonies and services to the congregation or merely to observe pilgrims visiting the abbey.

THE ABBEY RUINS
1924 76156

Here we see the south transept of the abbey before the restoration had taken place, with the spire of St Paul's in the background. The grass area in the foreground of the photograph is now the Garden of Remembrance. The west wall of the south transept is interesting, as it features Gothic hollow-walling in the middle storey. The earlier church of St Laurence is thought to have been sited near the south transept. William of Malmesbury in his 'De Gesta Pontificum' refers to the story of the scholar Johannes Scottus, who visited Malmesbury from France to teach the monks at the abbey. The monks are said to have murdered him with their writing quills because they were displeased with his views. This event may have actually taken place at the church of St Laurence.

THE ABBEY
The Interior, looking East c1947
M13501

Compare this view of the nave to the 1924 photograph. Above the altar we can see a decorated screen, which has long been removed. The long wooden pews of the earlier photograph have been replaced with chairs, and the chandeliers which were attached to the triforium are no longer in place. Notice the carved wooden pulpit, which was installed at the time of the restoration in 1928.

THE ABBEY, *The South Doorway c1955* M13019

The heavy outer walling of the south porch was added during the 14th century. The window above the porch belongs to the upper chamber or parvise, which in the 19th century was used as a schoolroom.

THE ABBEY, *The South Door c1955* M13025

The parvise above the south porch contains a small museum with various artefacts associated with the history of the abbey. Of particular interest are the four 15th-century beautifully illustrated and illuminated volumes of the Manuscript Bible. They were formerly at Cole Park, which had connections with the abbots of Malmesbury. They were purchased and presented to the abbey by the Earl of Suffolk and Berkshire in 1914.

THE ABBEY
c1955 M13005

Malmesbury Abbey has some superb architectural features. Below the windows on either side of the south porch, portions of the interlaced Norman arcading which ran between the buttresses can be seen. Surmounting all the walls and the south porch is a pierced parapet. Above this are fine pinnacles and flying buttresses.

THE ABBEY, *The South Front c1955* M13018

In the 14th century, alterations to the abbey were made. The small Norman windows were enlarged, the flat roof was vaulted, and the west end was rebuilt.

THE ABBEY
The West Front c1955
M13026

The west tower fell during the 17th century, causing considerable damage to the south-west corner of the nave. A wall was built across the nave at the west end. The original window had wooden tracery, but this was replaced in the early 19th century in stone. The building on the left is the Old Bell, at one time known as the Castle. The grounds of the Old Bell are thought to form part of the 12th-century castle built by Roger, Bishop of Salisbury. Archaeological excavations have taken place here in the past, but as yet the evidence is unsubstantiated.

THE ABBEY *c1955* M13036

Malmesbury Abbey has some interesting table tombs and gravestones. On the right as you come into the churchyard is a gravestone dedicated to Hannah Twynnoy. The epitaph tells the sad story of her untimely demise. It reads as follows:

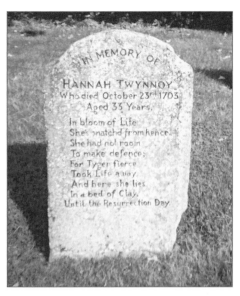

'In Memory of HANNAH TWYNNOY who died October 23rd 1703. Aged 33 Years.

In bloom of life

She's snatched from hence

She had not room

To make defence:

For Tyger fierce

Took life away

And here she lies

In a bed of clay

Until the Resurrection Day.'

Hannah was a maidservant at the White Lion Inn in Gloucester Street at the time that a travelling menagerie visited the inn. Legend suggests that she either teased the tiger or that the animal escaped and killed her.

HANNAH TWYNNOY'S GRAVESTONE
2004 ZZZ02075 (Photograph by R Prince)

THE ABBEY, *North Side c1955* M13015

In the foreground of this photograph we can see the Malmesbury Branch Railway line, which was opened in December 1877 by the GWR to link Malmesbury to Dauntsey station. The station was closed in 1962 and dismantled in 1963, like so many others during this time. In the background, the fine building adjacent to the abbey is abbey House, and to the south east is the water tower built in c1860 by the Malmesbury Water Works Co Ltd.

THE ABBOT'S HOUSE, MALMESBURY
after S H Grimm 1790
ZZZ02076
(Reproduced courtesy of the Athelstan Museum)

THE ABBEY *c1955* M13027

This pastoral scene includes the impressive Malmesbury Abbey on the skyline and abbey House, partly hidden behind the trees. Abbey House was built in the mid 16th century either by William Stumpe, who was a wealthy clothier in Malmesbury, or his eldest son, James. It was built on the remaining 13th-century vaulted undercroft of a monastic building which was part of the Benedictine abbey. At the Dissolution of the Monasteries the main building was demolished, and the abbey buildings were given to Sir Edward Baynton. Later William Stumpe, who was also a deputy for Sir Edward, purchased the abbey and the monastic buildings from the Crown. In the late 16th century, William Stumpe's second son John upgraded the house, and further alterations took place in the 19th and early 20th centuries. In the 1920s Harold Brakspear FSA undertook further improvements. A new wing at the east end was built for the owner of Abbey House, Captain E M Scott Mackirdy.

33

THE ABBEY
c1955 M13028

Compare this charming rural scene with the photograph taken in 1924 on page 20. The abbey mill is hidden behind the trees, and the farm buildings are overgrown. Corn grown on the common was taken to the abbey Mill to be ground into flour.

THE ABBEY
c1960 M13042

The Old Bell Hotel is situated on the left of the abbey. Behind the abbey to the north are the Cloister Gardens; these were created between 1979 and 1980 to celebrate the 1100 years of the charter which is believed to have been awarded in Saxon times.

THE ABBEY *c1960* M13055

The parvise above the south porch was believed to have been used as a gunpowder store during the Civil War in the 17th century. Evidence of damage has been found to the fabric of the abbey, which is possibly due to this storage.

THE ABBEY
c1960 M13072

Another fine window, designed by Morris & Co Ltd in the 19th century, can be seen in the south aisle situated in front of St Aldhelm's chapel. This memorial is dedicated to the Luce family, who were benefactors to the town, Members of Parliament, and owners of the abbey Brewery and the Mill Brewery. Many members of the family also served in the armed forces.

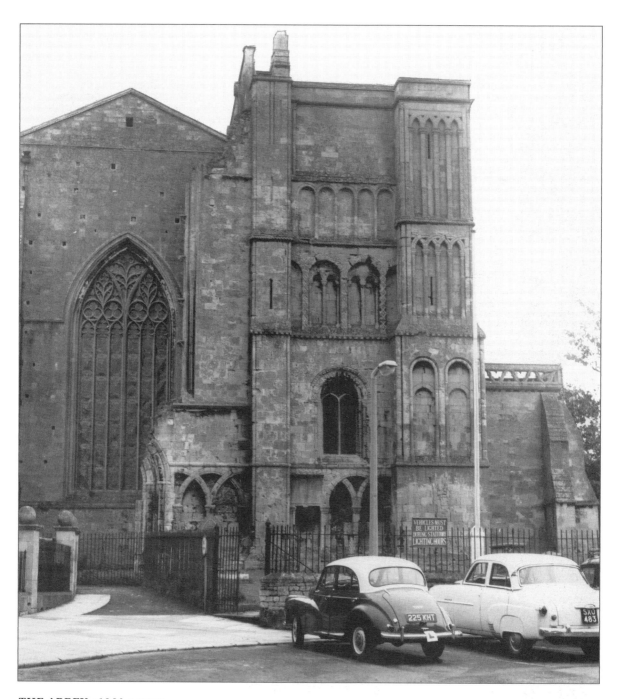

THE ABBEY *c1960* M13056

Within the vestry of the abbey at the south-west end are stained glass windows dating from 1928. They commemorate St Peter and St Paul and four historical characters linked with Malmesbury's past: Maildulph, St Aldhelm, William of Malmesbury, and the monk Eilmer, whose at flight in the 11th century is recorded by the historian William of Malmesbury.

THE ABBEY FROM THE WEST
AND THE OLD BELL *c1960* M13045

This is a similar photograph to the one taken in c1955 on page 31. But notice that the creeper covering the Old Bell has been removed around the entrance, exposing an attractive ornamental parapet. The pathway leads to the Cloister Gardens, to the north of the abbey.

detail of M13045

THE MARKET CROSS

THE OCTAGONAL limestone market cross was built during the reign of Henry VII in c1490; it has flying buttresses, pinnacles, and a vaulted interior, and it is surmounted by an octagonal turret. The turret has niches which contain various sculptured figures associated with Malmesbury's historical past. On the west face is the Crucifixion, and the other sculptures are reputed to be St Paul, the Madonna and Child, St Aldhelm, King Athelstan, Maildulph, St Laurence and St Peter. The market cross was restored in 1912 by Harold Brakspear FSA, and more recently in 1991, when conservation treatment was undertaken. The market cross had been damaged during the 1970s, when further pinnacles were repaired and replaced; one of the pinnacles which was not replaced is on display in the Athelstan Museum. Also in the museum is a fine drawing of the market cross by Thomas Girtin (c1790), featuring a market scene with people and trestle tables around the market cross. The drawing also shows the timber-framed vicarage in Gloucester Street, which was demolished in the late 19th century; the land became part of the adjoining White Lion Inn. The town well and stocks were situated by the market cross. Until the mid 20th century, Malmesbury was a market town, with a cattle market held on the third Wednesday of each month. During the early 13th century a Saturday market was also held, possibly near St Paul's parish church and later in Abbey Row. Between c1900 and 1940 a general market was held in the Cross Hayes. Various other markets and fairs were held in Malmesbury, notably on St Aldhelm's day celebrated on the 25th May, which was granted to Malmesbury Abbey by William I.

THE MARKET CROSS
A pencil drawing by Thomas Girtin 1790
ZZZ02056 (Reproduced courtesy of the Athelstan Museum)

Thomas Girtin (1775-1802) was a friend and contemporary of J M W Turner, and like Turner was an excellent watercolour painter and topographical artist. This pencil drawing of the market cross looks east from Gloucester Street towards Oxford Street. Thomas Girtin is reputed to have visited Malmesbury with J M W Turner on two occasions in the 1790s.

THE MARKET CROSS
A drawing by J Coney 1815
ZZZ02057
(Reproduced courtesy of the Athelstan Museum)

THE MARKET CROSS *1854*
ZZZ02058
(Photograph courtesy of the Athelstan Museum)

This early photograph of the market cross shows the position of the town stocks. At this date the hospital has not yet been built.

THE MARKET CROSS
1924 76145

The octagonal, vaulted market cross was built c1490, during the reign of Henry VII. John Leland, writing in 1542, states that the market cross was 'for poore market folkes to stand dry when Rayne cummith'. As we can see in this photograph, from the gentlemen gathered beneath the market cross, it was as good a place to meet in 1924 as it is today. The building behind the cars (right) is the abbey Café, which was the Green Dragon Inn from 1803 to1922.

THE MARKET CROSS *1924* 76146

On the left of the market cross is the turreted gateway of the Tolsey, also referred to as the Blind House or the Lock-up, built c1790. The passageway leads to Malmesbury Abbey. To the right of the market cross, and covered in creeper, is Malmesbury Cottage Hospital, which was opened in 1889 and rebuilt in 1897 incorporating the Prince and Princess Inn. The hospital moved in 1925 to the Manor House, Burton Hill.

THE MARKET CROSS *c1955* M13007

In this later photograph, there are inevitably more cars parked around the market cross. The building with the tall chimney stacks dates from the late 19th century; it was the Maternity Hospital and nursing home until the hospital moved to Burton Hill in 1925. At a much later date, in 1997, the Abbeyfield Society took over the premises and opened Abbeyfield House, providing sheltered accommodation for the elderley.

41

THE MARKET CROSS AND OXFORD STREET *c1955* M13017

We are looking down Oxford Street, with the market cross on the left. The tower of Tower House can be seen at the junction with Cross Hayes Lane (right). Tower House has a long and interesting history. The 19th-century tower, built by Dr Player for astronomical study, is incorporated into an older medieval house. William Stumpe, the wealthy clothier who had purchased the abbey and its monastic buildings from the Crown at the Dissolution of the Monasteries, is reputed to have entertained Henry VIII in the medieval banqueting hall, which also has a minstrels' gallery. The building was part of the poorhouse for the parish in the early 19th century. The tower was also used as an observatory during World War II by the Royal Observer Corps.

THE MARKET CROSS *c1955*
M13016

The Cottage Hospital situated by the market cross (right) has now become the offices for the Malmesbury Gas and Coke Company and premises for the Shamrock III Tea Rooms. When we compare this photograph with the one taken in 1924 (page 40 ref 76146), we can see that the creeper has now been cut and the building painted. On the east side of the High Street is the premises (with concealed overhead blinds) of Walter Jones, stationer, tobacconist, and hairdresser.

detail of M13016

THE MARKET CROSS *c1955* M13037

This photograph was taken from under the arch of the gateway leading to Malmesbury Abbey, looking out towards the market cross. The shop front visible at the top of the High Street is the Chippenham Co-op Society. This used to be the Red Lion public house in the late 18th century, and later in the 19th century, with a remodelled shop front, it became Frederick Newman & Sons, a grocer's.

THE MARKET CROSS FROM UNDERNEATH THE ABBEY GATEWAY *2004* ZZZ02059 (Photograph by R Prince)

THE MARKET CROSS
c1955 M13038

We are standing underneath the market cross and looking down the High Street. The road at this junction has traffic going in both directions, unlike today, when as part of the High Street one-way system the traffic now flows towards the market cross. On the right are some interesting directional AA road signs for Cricklade, Cirencester, Bristol and Gloucester. The finger sign points to a more essential local destination, as it reads 'Lavatories'. The shop beneath the signs is owned by Norman H Lewis, a watchmaker and jeweller. On the left, near the parked van, is a handsome red brick building with an 18th-century façade with later 19th-century parapet and architraves. The Rural District Council had their offices here from 1939 to 1964. Before this it was the premises for Brooke, a baker in the mid 19th century, and then a smaller Malmesbury bank which was taken over by North Wiltshire Banking Co. The premises were next occupied by the Capital and Counties Bank Ltd until 1924.

THE MARKET CROSS
c1955 M13039

To the right of the market cross is the Abbey Tea Rooms & Craft Shop owned by Hilda Long. Her name is on the sign above the parked car. The shop with the bicycle outside (to the left of the cross) is owned by Frederick Day, a butcher, and the shop opposite on the corner was possibly his fishmonger's and poulterer's shop. On the bend of the road and above the postern gate is a large mirror, erected in 1913 on behalf of the Countess of Suffolk and Berkshire, to enable the traffic to see around the sharp bend in Gloucester Street. The mirror is still positioned there today.

THE MARKET CROSS *c1960* M13073

Behind the market cross rises a spire, all that remains of St Paul's Parish Church, situated in Gloucester Street. The clock tower, which dates from the 14th century, was built on earlier foundations. By the 16th century the church had fallen into disrepair, and it had been demolished by the late 19th century. The bell tower and clock are still in use today. The original turret clock was made by Henry Weight in 1859; his business was situated in the High Street. The clock can now be seen in the Athelstan Museum.

THE MARKET CROSS *c1960* M13062

By the 1960s the addition of road markings indicating the one-way traffic system are now visible in the High Street, and road signs are positioned by the market cross. It appears that some event is taking place under the market cross, as there are advertising boards by the stall.

THE
HIGH STREET

IN THE PAST the High Street has been referred to as Magna Strata. The street is linked to other sections of the town by a series of lanes running west and east. To the west, and about halfway down the High Street, is the entrance to King's Wall, which joins the street at the site of the old south gate. To the east, other lanes link the High Street with Oxford Street, the Cross Hayes and Silver Street. The layout today is similar to that of the town during the 13th century.

THE MARKET CROSS AND THE ABBEY FROM THE HIGH STREET
1860 ZZZ02060 (Reproduced courtesy of the Athelstan Museum)

This lithograph of the market cross and the abbey was made by W Hanks, an artist and photographer of Malmesbury, from a pencil drawing by F Messiter dated 1818.

J R MAY'S SHOP, 18 HIGH STREET *1897* ZZZ02061 (Photograph courtesy of the Athelstan Museum)

Here we see J R May's shop decorated to celebrate Queen Victoria's Diamond Jubilee in 1897. The sign over the shop reads 'James May, Town Crier and Bill Poster'. The passageway to the left leads from the High Street through to the Cross Hayes; it was first known as May's Entry, and later as The Gant and then latterly as Griffin Alley.

F COMPTON, DRAPER

High Street 1887 ZZZ02062 (Photograph courtesy of the Athelstan Museum)

Frederick Compton's shop is decorated to celebrate Queen Victoria's Jubilee in 1887. Notice the shop window, which appears to be full of ostrich plumes.

HIGH STREET *1924* 76143

This view of the High Street shows Riddick, 'Printer, Bookbinder & Stationer', on the left. Next door, the shop with the wide bay window and the two people talking outside is the business of Thomas Bower & Son, whose draper's and outfitter's business was here from c1915 to 1927. The building is early 17th-century, and was re-fronted in 1849. The next shop is owned by the India & China Tea Co. Note how deserted the street is: there are no parked cars, except the one by the market cross.

HIGH STREET *1924*
76144

At the north end of the High Street stands the 15th-century market cross, with Malmesbury Cottage Hospital and the abbey in the background. On the left, the shop with the sign on top of the white window is the family business of Riddick, printers, bookbinders and stationers from 1911 to the 1970s. Next door, the imposing building with the red brick façade and advertisements is Jones & Sons, cycle agents and ironmongers. Mr James A Jones, the proprietor, was the mayor during 1924.

LOOKING TOWARDS THE HIGH STREET
c1955 M13020

This wonderful view of the market cross and the High Street was possibly taken from Malmesbury Abbey. On the left in the foreground is the rear view of what was once Malmesbury Cottage Hospital, but at this date it was the offices of the Malmesbury Gas & Coke Company and the Shamrock III tea rooms. On the far right is the turreted gateway leading to the abbey, the Blind House or the Lock-up built in the late 18th century, and known as the Tolsey.

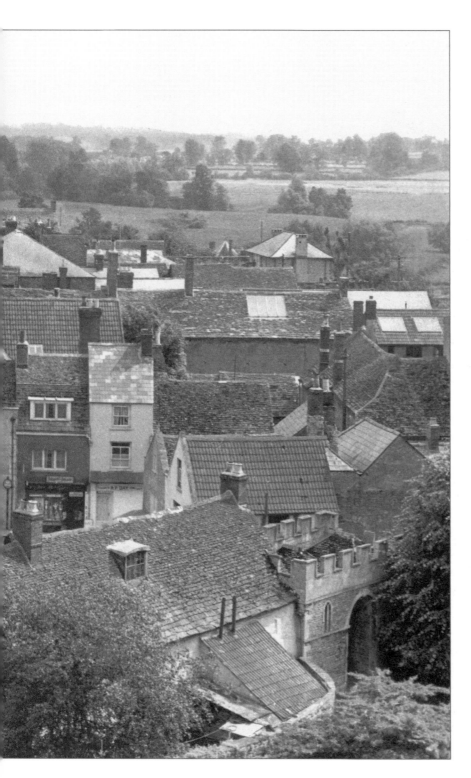

HIGH STREET FROM THE ABBEY ROOF
c1955 M13022

Taken from the abbey roof, this photograph shows the 15th-century market cross in the centre, situated at the north end of the High Street. There are no road markings on the road at this date. The undulating roofline of the houses in the High Street makes a very attractive scene.

HIGH STREET *c1960* M13070

Compare this photograph to the ones taken c1924. Notice that there is now a road sign on the left, by the Midland Bank, and that Boots has now replaced H W Bryan, the chemist. The motorcycle shop on the right has Shell and petrol signs, and on the front of the George Hotel (extreme right) are RAC and AA signs. The George was an 18th-century coaching inn, and

under the archway, through the wooden doors, was a cobbled carriageway which used to lead through to the Cross Hayes. It was a thriving hotel during the 19th and 20th centuries, but it closed in the late 1970s, when the premises were altered and became the George Veterinary Surgery. An interesting group of 1960s cars, including a Morris 1000 and a Morris 1000 Traveller, are parked by the market cross.

HIGH STREET *c1960* M13063

The King's Arms on the left (with the bicycle parked outside) probably dates from the late 17th century; note its timber-framed south window and jettied first floor. Further up the street on the same side, by the parked lorry, and with the black sign outside, is the Midland Bank, now the HSBC. This was previously the premises of the London County, City & Midland Bank between 1923 and 1927, and in the 19th century of Frederick Compton, a draper. On the right, with the petrol pumps outside, is E S T Cole, 'Motor Agent', whose business was on these premises from 1931 to 1980. Previously on these premises was a grocer, Henry Farrant; in 1927 the business was sold to the Adye family. The International Stores (extreme right) were operating between 1927 and 1985; before this, the business of Tom Brooke, a grocer and confectioner, had occupied the shop from 1889 to 1920.

HIGH STREET *c1960*
M13069

This is the southern end of the High Street, looking up towards the site of the south gate leading to King's Wall. The High Street has many 18th-century houses hidden behind the shop fronts. By the late 18th century and early 19th century, new building was taking place in the town.

HIGH STREET AND KING'S WALL *2004*
ZZZ02063 (Photograph by R Prince)

This photograph shows the entrance to King's Wall and the site of the south gate. King's Wall is reputed to be named after Matthew King, another wealthy 16th-century clothier from Malmesbury.

KING'S WALK *2004* ZZZ02064 (Photograph by R Prince)

This passageway leads from King's Wall through to the High Street, and was once known as the Tuppenny Tube.

THE KING'S ARMS *1924* 76148

The King's Arms, situated in the High Street, appears to have had
a long history, as it was opened in the late 17th century. By the
19th century the proprietor was Mr Henry (Harry) Jones, who was
a very well-known and respected gentleman of the town. The
description of him as jolly and a veritable John Bull character
fitted him very well. He was mayor of Malmesbury in 1895. His
style of dress was unique: he wore trousers turned up to his
ankles and a long loose-fitted coat over a colourful waistcoat, and
on his head a top hat (now in the Athelstan Museum). He
corresponded with various notable people, including royalty. He
was so well known that a letter addressed to him with simply a
drawing of his top hat and the word 'Wiltshire' written on the
envelope was delivered safely to him. When he died in August
1911 he was greatly mourned. The shop to the right of the King's
Arms is the business of Frederick William Yarnold, a watchmaker.

MR HENRY (HARRY) JONES
ZZZ02065 (Photograph courtesy of the Athelstan Museum, photographer M Brook)

Harry Jones was the proprietor of the King's Arms Hotel during the 19th century. The photograph shows his portrait and his famous top hat, and the various letters which were written to him. Also visible is the envelope sent to him with just a drawing of his hat and the word 'Wiltshire' written on the front.

AROUND MALMESBURY

THE PARISH of Malmesbury situated within the walls was called Byneport until the 16th century, and there was also the parish of Westport, which lay beyond the walls. In the late 19th century the civil parishes were created by dividing the municipal borough: they were Malmesbury St Paul's Within, Westport St Mary Within, the Abbey and Brokenborough Within. Later, by the mid 20th century, the parishes within the borough merged to form Malmesbury Parish, then St Paul's without was added along with other areas of Brokenborough. In the 1970s Malmesbury lost its borough status. In the 1980s the parish grew with more houses being built, for instance in the area of Burnivale.

THE ABBEY AND THE MARKET CROSS *1864* ZZZ02066 (Photograph courtesy of the Athelstan Museum)

ST PAUL'S CHURCH TOWER
c1955 M13021

This splendid photograph was taken from the abbey, and shows the remaining spire and clock tower of the former St Paul's Church. The original church dated from the 12th century. However, by the 16th century all that remained was the west tower and part of the east end. The east end was used as a Town Hall, and was possibly used by the old Corporation of Malmesbury during the 18th century. The spire and clock tower are 14th-century, and the belfry, which contains eight bells, is used in conjunction with services held in the abbey. The 19th-century clock mechanism was dismantled in the 1950s and an electrical unit was installed for operating the clock. Eventually in 1986 the turret clock was assembled and put on display in the Athelstan Museum.

THE MALMESBURY BRANCH RAILWAY *1876* ZZZ02067 (Photograph courtesy of the Athelstan Museum)

Here we see the GWR construction workmen working on the Malmesbury branch railway in 1876. The vertical boiler locomotive was known as the Coffee Pot.

THE MALMESBURY BRANCH RAILWAY *1905*

ZZZ02068 (Photograph courtesy of Athelstan Museum)

A train from Dauntsey arrives at Malmesbury Station. This photograph also shows the engine shed and the parcel office.

THE RIVER AVON AND THE RAILWAY FROM THE ABBEY ROOF *c1955* M13023

We are overlooking the Old Bell gardens and looking towards the river Avon and the Malmesbury Branch Railway. During the mid 19th century, proposals were put forward to build a railway line to connect the town with the south of England. The Wiltshire & Gloucestershire Railway Company put forward a bill to undertake the work, which was finally sanctioned on 21 June 1864. There were also negotiations between the W & GR, the GWR, and the Midland Railway. Progress was hindered by the hostile attitude between the GWR and the Midland Railway, but eventually a ceremony to cut the first sod of the W & GR was performed on 1 July 1865 by the Countess of Suffolk and Berkshire, using the silver-mounted ceremonial wheelbarrow which is now in the Athelstan Museum. Problems between the various railway companies were not resolved for a further few years, and the W & GR ceased to exist in 1871. Finally a branch line from the GWR line at Dauntsey to Malmesbury was opened in December 1877, linking the town to Paddington; the station was built east of the town. A spur was also built at Little Somerford, connecting the Malmesbury branch line to Bristol and South Wales. The railway was finally closed in November 1962 and dismantled in 1963.

THE SILVER-MOUNTED WHEELBARROW *1865* ZZZ02069 (Photograph courtesy of the Athelstan Museum)

This silver-mounted wheelbarrow (which is on display in the Athelstan Museum) was used by the Countess of Suffolk and Berkshire during the ceremony to cut the first sod of the Wiltshire & Gloucestershire Railway on 1 July 1865.

ABBEY ROW FROM THE ABBEY ROOF
c1955 M13024

The photograph shows Abbey Row; we are looking down towards the Triangle and the parish of Westport. The greenhouse behind the wall (centre foreground) was owned by the Old Bell; it was demolished in 1977 to enable the Queen's Jubilee Garden to be created, which was opened in 1978. By the garden is a flight of steps called Betty Geyser's (Gaze's) steps, which lead down to Burnivale. The west gate into the walled town is thought to have been situated near here. Damage is thought to have occurred to Abbey Row during the Civil War in 1643.

67

THE BELL INN
1913-14 ZZZ02070
(Photograph courtesy
of Wiltshire County
Council Museum
Service)

Messrs E S T Cole
Ltd's taxi fleet is
parked outside the
Bell Inn.

THE BELL INN *c1950*
M13010

The Bell Inn, as it was
called at this time, was
once called the Castle in
the 18th century. The shop
opposite (left) is possibly
owned by H C Avis, a florist.

THE OLD BELL *c1960* M13041

The Bell Inn has now been renamed the Old Bell. The eastern part of the building was extended to incorporate other dwellings. One was Castle House, whose owner, Joseph Moore, was licensee of The Old Bell and mayor of Malmesbury in 1894 and in 1909. The other house was owned by Mrs White, who sold hats and bonnets in the 19th Century. To the west of the Old Bell is Mill Lane, leading to the abbey mill which was owned by the abbey.

THE OLD BELL
c1960 M13048

The interior of the Old Bell has some very interesting architectural features. The inn may originally have been part of the castle built in c1130 by Bishop Roger of Salisbury, although archaeological investigations have not substantiated this. The Crown gave the castle to the abbey in 1215, and by 1216 a licence was given to demolish it and allow the abbey to build on the site. In the museum is a photograph of the medieval wall paintings which are to be found in the loft of the inn on either side of the chimney breast.

THE OLD BELL GARDENS *c1960* M13049

This beautiful garden features ornamental box hedging in a design similar to an Elizabethan maze or knot garden. Here it is planted with flowers. Today the hedges are taller, with a narrow gravel path between them.

THE OLD BELL HOTEL GARDENS *c1960* M13050

This elevated view of the garden shows the gazebo at the end of the garden. The garden walls to the north are part of the town wall defences.

THE VIEW FROM DANIEL'S WELL
c1955 M13011

The pathway to the right leads back to Daniel's Well. Beyond the trees is the River Avon, and the houses in the distance are in Bristol Street and part of Burnivale. The spire of the Congregational church in Westport can be seen on the skyline.

THE VIEW FROM DANIEL'S WELL
c1955 M13009

Near the trees flows the spring waters of Daniel's Well, which is named after a bishop of Malmesbury Abbey who lived during the 8th century. He is reputed to have bathed in the waters. In the distance, high on the hill, stands the abbey, and to the west is the Old Bell Hotel. Beyond the stream, the River Avon flows towards the Mill Brewery, also called the Maltings; it was originally owned by C R Luce, and later became the Linolite Limited factory between 1941 and 1984. By 1958 Linolite Limited had purchased the property. The company designed and manufactured electric light fittings and signs. The director of the company invented the filament tubular electric lamp system in 1901, and the company specialised in the field of strip lighting.

THE RIVER AVON FROM DANIEL'S WELL *c1955* M13012

Malmesbury is virtually surrounded by the two tributaries of the River Avon. This branch of the river passes through the Mill Brewery, at this time owned by Linolite Limited, and on to the weir by St John's Bridge and the Avon Mill, eventually joining the other tributary, the Tetbury Avon, at Wyniard Mill.

THE WAR MEMORIAL AND WESTPORT POST OFFICE
c1950 M13014

The war memorial is built on the site of the old weighbridge, and was dedicated in a ceremony held in 1921. The van parked by the Gothic-style Methodist church (left) belongs to W Redman & Sons, the butchers, whose premises are next door to G H Handy, a tobacconist's, which was once Westport Post Office. The sign over the shop front by the window is advertising cigarettes. The premises returned to being a sub-post office in 1996.

THE TRIANGLE AND THE WAR MEMORIAL *c1955* M13033

A 1930s telephone box stands outside the Three Cups Inn (centre right). This inn is one of the 17th-century buildings in Westport to survive the Civil War skirmishes between the Royalists and the Parliamentary forces lead by Sir William Waller. Legend states that he may have made the inn his headquarters. The lane to the left of the inn is Katifer Lane, whose name is derived from the Norman-French word 'kat', meaning cloth, and 'fer' meaning iron - thus Katifer Lane was the street of the cloth ironers. Malmesbury was an important centre in the 16th century for the woollen cloth industry, and was famous for producing woollen broadcloth. The spire behind the inn belongs to the Congregational Church.

THE TRIANGLE *c1960* M13057

This area of Malmesbury was once called the Sheep Fair; it is in the parish of Westport, which by the late 19th century became a civil parish of westport St Mary Within. Westport was separated from Malmesbury as it was situated outside the west gate to the town, and it was linked to the town by Abbey Row. Burnivale and King's Wall are included in the parish of Westport.

THE TRIANGLE
c1960 M13061

The road to the right of the Three Cups Inn is St Mary's Street. St Mary's Church Hall on the right was built on the Anglo-Saxon foundations of St Mary's of Westport Church, which was destroyed at the time of the Civil War in the 17th century, possibly by Sir William Waller. It underwent rebuilding in both the 18th and 19th centuries. Thomas Hobbes (1588-1679), the famous philosopher, was born in Malmesbury in a house near Westport church, which is no longer extant.

THE CONGREGATIONAL CHURCH *c1960* M13060

In the 1870s a new Congregational chapel is mentioned in Westport. The chapel also had a schoolroom. An earlier church was here in the 18th century. The chapel became the United Reformed Church in 1994.

BURNIVALE *c1955* M13031

To the right of this pathway is another which leads to the site of the postern gate, which was part of the early 11th- and 12th-century defences of Malmesbury. The steps lead down to the Linolite factory, which incorporated C R Luce's brewery, and the Postern Mill (which was irresponsibly demolished in 1984). Behind the wall, near the cottage being painted white, is a path leading to Daniel's Well. Opposite the cottages on the left (beyond the wall on the right), is the area where the early Hermitage may have stood, below the walls, under St Paul's spire. A pencil drawing of the Hermitage by J Carter dated 1801 is in the British Museum. Christine of Somerford was enclosed in the Hermitage in the mid 13th century. A building known as the Hermitage was demolished in the 19th century. Nowadays, the area has changed. The growth of a tree obscures the view towards Burnivale, although the spire of the Congregational church (now the United Reformed Church) can still be seen in the distance. Houses, known as the Maltings, were built in the 1980s on the site of the Linolite factory.

BURNIVALE
2004 ZZZ02071
(Photograph by R Prince)

The steps lead up to the site of the postern gate and into Gloucester Street.

BURNIVALE
2004 ZZZ02072
(Photograph by R Prince)

Here we see cottages in Burnivale with St Paul's spire in the distance.

THE RIVER AVON
c1955 M13029

The River Avon has played a very important part in the town's industrial history, and particularly in the woollen industry. The Tetbury Avon, which flows from the north-east of the town, was also known as the Ingleburne. Both branches of the river meet near Wyniard Mill.

BASKERVILLE
c1955 M13030

Here the River Avon flows under Goose Bridge. This steep old bridge was unfortunately modernised in the late 1960s, but the medieval cutwaters underneath still remain. Beyond the bridge is Back Hill Steps. Behind the cottages near the steps is a large three-storey house with gables. This is Culver House, which once housed the servants for the manor house and also a pigeon or dove cote - the pigeons were bred for the lord of the manor's table.

THE RIVER *c1960* M13067

We are still in Baskerville, looking in the opposite direction to photograph M13030, with Goose Bridge to the extreme left of the photograph. The pathway and river lead to Wyniard Mill (on the far left), which was a cloth mill in the late 16th to the early 17th century. A dye house and two corn mills were there by the mid 17th century. The mill was once owned by Malmesbury Abbey before the Dissolution.

BACK HILL STEPS
c1960 M13068

Back Hill Steps ascend steeply towards the site of one of the town gates which formed part of the early defences of the town. The gate has been referred to by different names: Wyniard's Gate, Small Gate, or Little Gate. Parts of the town wall defences were restored during the 18th and 19th centuries. The walls were constructed in three phases between the 7th and the 12th centuries – there had been earlier timber defences during the Iron Age and Saxon times. Back Hill Steps continues up towards Silver Street and the Cross Hayes.

CELEBRATING QUEEN VICTORIA'S JUBILEE IN THE CROSS HAYES
1887 ZZZ02073
(Photograph courtesy of the Athelstan Museum)

THE CROSS HAYES AND THE TOWN HALL *2004*
ZZZ02074 (Photograph by R Prince)

Today the Cross Hayes is a car park. The Town Hall, which is the Civic Centre for the community, also contains the offices for the Town Council and Tourist Information. The Athelstan Museum is situated through the double wooden doors.

THE ALMSHOUSES
1924 76147

The Hospital of the Order of St John the Baptist is situated at the junction of the Lower High Street and St John's Street and by St John's Bridge. The entrance to the hospital was through the medieval arched doorway. Above this doorway is an inscription describing the endowments given by the aldermen and burgesses of the Borough of Malmesbury to maintain the free school and almshouses. The date of the foundation of the hospital is uncertain, but the hospital was mentioned in the 13th- and 14th-century rentals of Malmesbury Abbey as having paid 2s 8¾d for the site. A prior with brethren and sisters cared for the sick. The building was an almshouse in 1622.

THE RIVER *c1960* M13064

We are standing on St John's Bridge and overlooking the River Avon, with the Avon Mill on the right. The bridge was also referred to as Mill Bridge.

THE RIVER AND THE BRIDGE *c1960* M13065

St John's Bridge is on the left. The Avon Mill at this time was occupied by Hugh Dryden & Co Ltd, who sold antiques and works of art here until the late 1970s. In the 17th century an earlier fulling mill, called Cannop's Mill, stood on the site. This was purchased by Francis Hill who built the Burton Hill Mill (Avon Mill), which became a cloth mill producing fine broadcloth. The mill was enlarged in the early 19th century. By the 1830s the mill briefly became a corn mill (grist mill), returning to broadcloth production when the Salter family had the mill. Woollen broadcloth continued to be produced here during the 1840s, and was dyed and finished at Cowbridge Mill. Silk ribbon was manufactured when the mill was taken over by Thomas Bridget & Co of Derby in the mid 19th century; the mill continued to operate under various owners, including Joseph Davenport & Sons and the Wiltshire Silk Manufacturing Co, and from 1923 to 1939 it was known as the Avon Silk Mill. The silk mill employed mainly women and girls. Liberty silk was made at the mill until the start of World War II. Avon Mill was eventually sold, and it was converted into flats by 1986.

THE HOSPITAL
c1955 M13003

Malmesbury Hospital, which was formerly the manor house, was rebuilt in the Tudor style in the late 19th century. The Cottage Hospital moved here in 1925 from its original premises situated by the market cross.

BURTON HILL HOUSE SCHOOL FOR CRIPPLED GIRLS
c1955 M13001

The original Burton Hill House was burned down in the 1840s. The old fire pump in the Athelstan Museum (see photograph below) is reputed to have attended the fire. The house, which was rebuilt in the Tudor Gothic style, was used to house evacuees during World War II. It was purchased by the Shaftesbury Society in 1945 and became Burton Hill School for handicapped children.

MALMESBURY FIRE BRIGADE *c1910* ZZZ02077 (Photograph courtesy of the Athelstan Museum)

The fire brigade, with the horse-drawn manual and crew and the old 18th-century hand-drawn fire pump on a cart, are possibly taking part in a procession.

BURTON HILL HOUSE SCHOOL FOR CRIPPLED GIRLS *c1955* M13002

Before the fire in the 1840s, the earlier Burton Hill House was owned by Edmund Estcourt, and in the late 18th century it was owned by the Avon Mill owner, Francis Hill. In the mid 19th century the estate and house was sold to C W Miles, and later in 1945 to the Shaftesbury Society for handicapped children.

BREMILHAM SCHOOL *c1960* M13059

This Secondary Modern school was opened in 1954 as an addition to the established Grammar School that was opened in 1903. The school also provided extra secretarial and other commercial courses, giving the pupils an alternative to the Higher Certificate taken at the Grammar School. There were facilities for 500 pupils.

THE BOWLING GREEN *c1960* M13066

The Malmesbury Bowling Club, which is in St John's Street, is on the same site today. It is situated close to the Goose Bridge in the Baskerville area of Malmesbury.

INDEX

Frith Book Co Titles

www.francisfrith.co.uk

The Frith Book Company publishes over 100 new titles each year. A selection of those currently available is listed below. For latest catalogue please contact Frith Book Co.
Town Books 96 pages, approximately 100 photos. **County and Themed Books** 128 pages, approximately 150 photos (unless specified). All titles hardback with laminated case and jacket, except those indicated pb (paperback)

Amersham, Chesham & Rickmansworth (pb)	1-85937-340-2	£9.99	Derbyshire Living Memories	1-85937-330-5	£14.99
Andover (pb)	1-85937-292-9	£9.99	Devon Churches (pb)	1-85937-250-3	£9.99
Aylesbury (pb)	1-85937-227-9	£9.99	Dorchester (pb)	1-85937-307-0	£9.99
Barnstaple (pb)	1-85937-300-3	£9.99	Dorset (pb)	1-85937-269-4	£9.99
Basildon Living Memories (pb)	1-85937-515-4	£9.99	Down the Severn (pb)	1-85937-560-x	£9.99
Bath (pb)	1-85937-419-0	£9.99	Down The Thames (pb)	1-85937-278-3	£9.99
Bedford (pb)	1-85937-205-8	£9.99	Down the Trent	1-85937-311-9	£14.99
Bedfordshire Living Memories	1-85937-513-8	£14.99	East Anglia (pb)	1-85937-265-1	£9.99
Belfast (pb)	1-85937-303-8	£9.99	East Grinstead (pb)	1-85937-138-8	£9.99
Berkshire (pb)	1-85937-191-4	£9.99	East Sussex (pb)	1-85937-606-1	£9.99
Berkshire Churches	1-85937-170-1	£17.99	Eastbourne (pb)	1-85937-399-2	£9.99
Berkshire Living Memories	1-85937-332-1	£14.99	Edinburgh (pb)	1-85937-193-0	£8.99
Blackpool (pb)	1-85937-393-3	£9.99	Essex - Second Selection	1-85937-456-5	£14.99
Bognor Regis (pb)	1-85937-431-x	£9.99	Essex (pb)	1-85937-270-8	£9.99
Bournemouth (pb)	1-85937-545-6	£9.99	Essex Coast	1-85937-342-9	£14.99
Bradford (pb)	1-85937-204-x	£9.99	Essex Living Memories	1-85937-490-5	£14.99
Bridgend (pb)	1-85937-386-0	£7.99	Exeter	1-85937-539-1	£9.99
Bridgwater (pb)	1-85937-305-4	£9.99	Exmoor (pb)	1-85937-608-8	£9.99
Bridport (pb)	1-85937-327-5	£9.99	Falmouth (pb)	1-85937-594-4	£9.99
Brighton (pb)	1-85937-192-2	£8.99	Folkestone (pb)	1-85937-124-8	£9.99
Bristol (pb)	1-85937-264-3	£9.99	Frome (pb)	1-85937-317-8	£9.99
British Life A Century Ago (pb)	1-85937-213-9	£9.99	Glamorgan	1-85937-488-3	£14.99
Buckinghamshire (pb)	1-85937-200-7	£9.99	Glasgow (pb)	1-85937-190-6	£9.99
Camberley (pb)	1-85937-222-8	£9.99	Glastonbury (pb)	1-85937-338-0	£7.99
Cambridge (pb)	1-85937-422-0	£9.99	Gloucester (pb)	1-85937-232-5	£9.99
Cambridgeshire (pb)	1-85937-420-4	£9.99	Gloucestershire (pb)	1-85937-561-8	£9.99
Cambridgeshire Villages	1-85937-523-5	£14.99	Greater Manchester (pb)	1-85937-266-x	£9.99
Canals And Waterways (pb)	1-85937-291-0	£9.99	Guildford (pb)	1-85937-410-7	£9.99
Canterbury Cathedral (pb)	1-85937-179-5	£9.99	Hampshire (pb)	1-85937-279-1	£9.99
Carmarthenshire (pb)	1-85937-604-5	£9.99	Harrogate (pb)	1-85937-423-9	£9.99
Chelmsford (pb)	1-85937-310-0	£9.99	Hastings and Bexhill (pb)	1-85937-131-0	£9.99
Cheltenham (pb)	1-85937-095-0	£9.99	Heart of Lancashire (pb)	1-85937-197-3	£9.99
Cheshire (pb)	1-85937-271-6	£9.99	Helston (pb)	1-85937-214-7	£9.99
Chester (pb)	1-85937-382-8	£9.99	Hereford (pb)	1-85937-175-2	£9.99
Chesterfield (pb)	1-85937-378-x	£9.99	Herefordshire (pb)	1-85937-567-7	£9.99
Chichester (pb)	1-85937-228-7	£9.99	Herefordshire Living Memories	1-85937-514-6	£14.99
Churches of East Cornwall (pb)	1-85937-249-x	£9.99	Hertfordshire (pb)	1-85937-247-3	£9.99
Churches of Hampshire (pb)	1-85937-207-4	£9.99	Horsham (pb)	1-85937-432-8	£9.99
Cinque Ports & Two Ancient Towns	1-85937-492-1	£14.99	Humberside (pb)	1-85937-605-3	£9.99
Colchester (pb)	1-85937-188-4	£8.99	Hythe, Romney Marsh, Ashford (pb)	1-85937-256-2	£9.99
Cornwall Living Memories	1-85937-248-1	£14.99	Ipswich (pb)	1-85937-424-7	£9.99
Cotswolds (pb)	1-85937-230-9	£9.99	Isle of Man (pb)	1-85937-268-6	£9.99
Cotswolds Living Memories	1-85937-255-4	£14.99	Isle of Wight (pb)	1-85937-429-8	£9.99
County Durham (pb)	1-85937-398-4	£9.99	Isle of Wight Living Memories	1-85937-304-6	£14.99
Croydon Living Memories (pb)	1-85937-162-0	£9.99	Kent (pb)	1-85937-189-2	£9.99
Derby (pb)	1-85937-367-4	£9.99	Kent Living Memories(pb)	1-85937-401-8	£9.99
Derbyshire (pb)	1-85937-196-5	£9.99	Kings Lynn (pb)	1-85937-334-8	£9.99

Available from your local bookshop or from the publisher

Frith Book Co Titles (continued)

Leicester (pb)	1-85937-381-x	£9.99	Sherborne (pb)	1-85937-301-1	£9.99
Leicestershire & Rutland Living Memories	1-85937-500-6	£12.99	Shrewsbury (pb)	1-85937-325-9	£9.99
Leicestershire (pb)	1-85937-185-x	£9.99	Shropshire (pb)	1-85937-326-7	£9.99
Lighthouses	1-85937-257-0	£9.99	Shropshire Living Memories	1-85937-643-6	£14.99
Lincoln (pb)	1-85937-380-1	£9.99	South Devon Living Memories (pb)	1-85937-609-6	£9.99
Lincolnshire (pb)	1-85937-433-6	£9.99	South East London (pb)	1-85937-263-5	£9.99
Liverpool and Merseyside (pb)	1-85937-234-1	£9.99	South Somerset	1-85937-318-6	£14.99
London (pb)	1-85937-183-3	£9.99	South Wales	1-85937-519-7	£14.99
London Living Memories	1-85937-454-9	£14.99	Southampton (pb)	1-85937-427-1	£9.99
Ludlow (pb)	1-85937-176-0	£9.99	Southport (pb)	1-85937-425-5	£9.99
Luton (pb)	1-85937-235-x	£9.99	St Albans (pb)	1-85937-341-0	£9.99
Maidenhead (pb)	1-85937-339-9	£9.99	St Ives (pb)	1-85937-415-8	£9.99
Maidstone (pb)	1-85937-391-7	£9.99	Stafford Living Memories (pb)	1-85937-503-0	£9.99
Marlborough (pb)	1-85937-336-4	£9.99	Staffordshire (pb)	1-85937-308-9	£9.99
Middlesex	1-85937-158-2	£14.99	Stourbridge (pb)	1-85937-530-8	£9.99
Monmouthshire	1-85937-532-4	£14.99	Stratford upon Avon (pb)	1-85937-388-7	£9.99
New Forest (pb)	1-85937-390-9	£9.99	Suffolk (pb)	1-85937-221-x	£9.99
Newark (pb)	1-85937-366-6	£9.99	Suffolk Coast (pb)	1-85937-610-x	£9.99
Newquay (pb)	1-85937-421-2	£9.99	Surrey (pb)	1-85937-240-6	£9.99
Norfolk (pb)	1-85937-195-7	£9.99	Surrey Living Memories	1-85937-328-3	£14.99
Norfolk Broads	1-85937-486-7	£14.99	Sussex (pb)	1-85937-184-1	£9.99
Norfolk Living Memories (pb)	1-85937-402-6	£9.99	Sutton (pb)	1-85937-337-2	£9.99
North Buckinghamshire	1-85937-626-6	£14.99	Swansea (pb)	1-85937-167-1	£9.99
North Devon Living Memories	1-85937-261-9	£14.99	Taunton (pb)	1-85937-314-3	£9.99
North Hertfordshire	1-85937-547-2	£14.99	Tees Valley & Cleveland (pb)	1-85937-623-1	£9.99
North London (pb)	1-85937-403-4	£9.99	Teignmouth (pb)	1-85937-370-4	£7.99
North Somerset	1-85937-302-x	£14.99	Thanet (pb)	1-85937-116-7	£9.99
North Wales (pb)	1-85937-298-8	£9.99	Tiverton (pb)	1-85937-178-7	£9.99
North Yorkshire (pb)	1-85937-236-8	£9.99	Torbay (pb)	1-85937-597-9	£9.99
Northamptonshire Living Memories	1-85937-529-4	£14.99	Truro (pb)	1-85937-598-7	£9.99
Northamptonshire	1-85937-150-7	£14.99	Victorian & Edwardian Dorset	1-85937-254-6	£14.99
Northumberland	1-85937-522-7	£14.99	Victorian & Edwardian Kent (pb)	1-85937-624-X	£9.99
Norwich (pb)	1-85937-194-9	£8.99	Victorian & Edwardian Maritime Album (pb)	1-85937-622-3	£9.99
Nottingham (pb)	1-85937-324-0	£9.99	Victorian and Edwardian Sussex (pb)	1-85937-625-8	£9.99
Nottinghamshire (pb)	1-85937-187-6	£9.99	Villages of Devon (pb)	1-85937-293-7	£9.99
Oxford (pb)	1-85937-411-5	£9.99	Villages of Kent (pb)	1-85937-294-5	£9.99
Oxfordshire (pb)	1-85937-430-1	£9.99	Warrington (pb)	1-85937-507-3	£9.99
Oxfordshire Living Memories	1-85937-525-1	£14.99	Warwick (pb)	1-85937-518-9	£9.99
Paignton (pb)	1-85937-374-7	£7.99	Welsh Castles (pb)	1-85937-322-4	£9.99
Peak District (pb)	1-85937-280-5	£9.99	West Yorkshire (pb)	1-85937-201-5	£9.99
Penzance (pb)	1-85937-595-2	£9.99	Weymouth (pb)	1-85937-209-0	£9.99
Peterborough (pb)	1-85937-219-8	£9.99	Wiltshire (pb)	1-85937-277-5	£9.99
Picturesque Harbours	1-85937-208-2	£14.99	Wiltshire Churches (pb)	1-85937-171-x	£9.99
Piers	1-85937-237-6	£17.99	Wiltshire Living Memories (pb)	1-85937-396-8	£9.99
Plymouth (pb)	1-85937-389-5	£9.99	Winchester (pb)	1-85937-428-x	£9.99
Poole & Sandbanks (pb)	1-85937-251-1	£9.99	Windsor (pb)	1-85937-333-x	£9.99
Redhill to Reigate (pb)	1-85937-596-0	£9.99	Wokingham & Bracknell (pb)	1-85937-329-1	£9.99
Ringwood (pb)	1-85937-384-4	£7.99	Woodbridge (pb)	1-85937-498-0	£9.99
Romford (pb)	1-85937-319-4	£9.99	Worcester (pb)	1-85937-165-5	£9.99
Royal Tunbridge Wells (pb)	1-85937-504-9	£9.99	York (pb)	1-85937-199-x	£9.99
Salisbury (pb)	1-85937-239-2	£9.99	Yorkshire (pb)	1-85937-186-8	£9.99
Scarborough (pb)	1-85937-379-8	£9.99	Yorkshire Coastal Memories	1-85937-506-5	£14.99
Sevenoaks and Tonbridge (pb)	1-85937-392-5	£9.99	Yorkshire Dales	1-85937-502-2	£14.99

See Frith books on the internet at www.francisfrith.co.uk

FRITH PRODUCTS & SERVICES

Francis Frith would doubtless be pleased to know that the pioneering publishing venture he started in 1860 still continues today. Over a hundred and forty years later, The Francis Frith Collection continues in the same innovative tradition and is now one of the foremost publishers of vintage photographs in the world. Some of the current activities include:

Interior Decoration

Today Frith's photographs can be seen framed and as giant wall murals in thousands of pubs, restaurants, hotels, banks, retail stores and other public buildings throughout the country. In every case they enhance the unique local atmosphere of the places they depict and provide reminders of gentler days in an increasingly busy and frenetic world.

Product Promotions

Frith products are used by many major companies to promote the sales of their own products or to reinforce their own history and heritage. Frith promotions have been used by Hovis bread, Courage beers, Scots Porage Oats, Colman's mustard, Cadbury's foods, Mellow Birds coffee, Dunhill pipe tobacco, Guinness, and Bulmer's Cider.

Genealogy and Family History

As the interest in family history and roots grows world-wide, more and more people are turning to Frith's photographs of Great Britain for images of the towns, villages and streets where their ancestors lived; and, of course, photographs of the churches and chapels where their ancestors were christened, married and buried are an essential part of every genealogy tree and family album.

Frith Products

All Frith photographs are available Framed or just as Mounted Prints and Posters (size 23 x 16 inches). These may be ordered from the address below. From time to time other products - Address Books, Maps, etc - are available.

The Internet

Already fifty thousand Frith photographs can be viewed and purchased on the internet through the Frith websites and a myriad of partner sites.

For more detailed information on Frith companies and products, look at these sites:

www.francisfrith.co.uk
www.francisfrith.com
(for North American visitors)

See the complete list of Frith Books at:

www.francisfrith.co.uk

This web site is regularly updated with the latest list of publications from the Frith Book Company. If you wish to buy books relating to another part of the country that your local bookshop does not stock, you may purchase on-line.

For further information, trade, or author enquiries please contact us at the address below:
The Francis Frith Collection, Frith's Barn, Teffont, Salisbury, Wiltshire, England SP3 5QP.
Tel: +44 (0)1722 716 376 Fax: +44 (0)1722 716 881 Email: sales@francisfrith.co.uk

See Frith books on the internet at www.francisfrith.co.uk

FREE PRINT OF YOUR CHOICE

Mounted Print
Overall size 14 x 11 inches (355 x 280mm)

Choose any Frith photograph in this book.
Simply complete the Voucher opposite and return it with your remittance for £2.25 (to cover postage and handling) and we will print the photograph of your choice in SEPIA (size 11 x 8 inches) and supply it in a cream mount with a burgundy rule line (overall size 14 x 11 inches).
Please note: photographs with a reference number starting with a "Z" are not Frith photographs and cannot be supplied under this offer.
Offer valid for delivery to one UK address only.

PLUS: Order additional Mounted Prints at HALF PRICE - £7.49 each (normally £14.99)
If you would like to order more Frith prints from this book, possibly as gifts for friends and family, you can buy them at half price (with no additional postage and handling costs).

PLUS: Have your Mounted Prints framed
For an extra £14.95 per print you can have your mounted print(s) framed in an elegant polished wood and gilt moulding, overall size 16 x 13 inches (no additional postage and handling required).

IMPORTANT!

These special prices are only available if you use this form to order . You must use the ORIGINAL VOUCHER on this page (no copies permitted). We can only despatch to one UK address. This offer cannot be combined with any other offer.

Send completed Voucher form to:
The Francis Frith Collection, Frith's Barn, Teffont, Salisbury, Wiltshire SP3 5QP

CHOOSE A PHOTOGRAPH FROM THIS BOOK

Voucher for **FREE** *and Reduced Price Frith Prints*

Please do not photocopy this voucher. Only the original is valid, so please fill it in, cut it out and return it to us with your order.

Picture ref no	Page no	Qty	Mounted @ £7.49	Framed + £14.95	Total Cost £
		1	Free of charge*	£	£
			£7.49	£	£
			£7.49	£	£
			£7.49	£	£
			£7.49	£	£
			£7.49	£	£

Please allow 28 days for delivery.
Offer available to one UK address only

* Post & handling	£2.25
Total Order Cost	£

Title of this book . . . .

I enclose a cheque/postal order for £ . . . .
made payable to 'The Francis Frith Collection'

OR please debit my Mastercard / Visa / Maestro / Amex card, details below

Card Number

Issue No (Maestro only)   Valid from (Maestro)

Expires   Signature

Name Mr/Mrs/Ms . . . .

Address . . . .

. . . .

. . . .

. . . . Postcode . . . .

Daytime Tel No . . . .

Email . . . .

Would you like to find out more about Francis Frith?

We have recently recruited some entertaining speakers who are happy to visit local groups, clubs and societies to give an illustrated talk documenting Frith's travels and photographs. If you are a member of such a group and are interested in hosting a presentation, we would love to hear from you.

Our speakers bring with them a small selection of our local town and county books, together with sample prints. They are happy to take orders. A small proportion of the order value is donated to the group who have hosted the presentation. The talks are therefore an excellent way of fundraising for small groups and societies.

Can you help us with information about any of the Frith photographs in this book?

We are gradually compiling an historical record for each of the photographs in the Frith archive. It is always fascinating to find out the names of the people shown in the pictures, as well as insights into the shops, buildings and other features depicted.

If you recognize anyone in the photographs in this book, or if you have information not already included in the author's caption, do let us know. We would love to hear from you, and will try to publish it in future books or articles.

Our production team

Frith books are produced by a small dedicated team at offices in the converted Grade II listed 18th-century barn at Teffont near Salisbury, illustrated above. Most have worked with the Frith Collection for many years. All have in common one quality: they have a passion for the Frith Collection. The team is constantly expanding, but currently includes:

Paul Baron, Phillip Brennan, Jason Buck, John Buck, Ruth Butler, Heather Crisp, David Davies, Louis du Mont, Isobel Hall, Gareth Harris, Lucy Hart, Julian Hight, Peter Horne, James Kinnear, Karen Kinnear, Tina Leary, Stuart Login, David Marsh, Lesley-Ann Millard, Sue Molloy, Glenda Morgan, Wayne Morgan, Sarah Roberts, Kate Rotondetto, Dean Scource, Eliza Sackett, Terence Sackett, Sandra Sampson, Adrian Sanders, Sandra Sanger, Jan Scrivens, Julia Skinner, David Smith, Miles Smith, Lewis Taylor, Shelley Tolcher, Lorraine Tuck, Amanita Wainwright and Ricky Williams.

Free Print – see overleaf